CONVERSATIONS
NOT CODE

**By: Rev. Dr. Joe Mucha,
Doctor of NLP Prompt Engineering**

CONVERSATIONS NOT CODE

TABLE OF CONTENTS

INTRODUCTION

Imagine a future where you converse with your computer, not in the strict, rigid syntax of code, but in the fluid, dynamic language of human conversation. A future where technology anticipates your needs, understands your requests, and assists you in tasks ranging from the mundane to the incredibly complex.

A future where your productivity is not limited by your programming skills, but amplified by your creativity and human insight. Welcome to the world of Conversations Not Code.

This book is your window into that future, a lens through which you can understand the present and glimpse the breathtaking potential of what's to come. With the advent of artificial intelligence (AI), particularly its subset Natural Language Processing (NLP), we are at the precipice of a revolution.

A revolution where machines not only understand our language but can generate human-like text, answer complex questions, write emails or reports, schedule meetings, and much more.

AI is not merely a tool, it is becoming our companion, our assistant, an extension of our intelligence. It holds the potential to reshape our world, just as the wheel, the printing press, electricity, and the internet have done in their times.

This revolution is not in the distant future; it's here and now, and it's accelerating at a pace that is both thrilling and challenging to keep up with.

But don't let the technical jargon intimidate you. At its core, AI is about people. It's about augmenting our capabilities, enhancing our efficiency, and giving us the power to do more with less. AI is not here to replace us; it's here to empower us.

This is the key message of this book: AI is fantastic. It's set to help everyone, in every job, become faster, better, and more productive. And the bridge that will bring us into this AI-augmented world is being built with Conversations Not Code.

We stand at a unique juncture in history, a pivot point where the promises of science fiction are becoming the possibilities of science fact. In the chapters that follow, we will walk through this dynamic, rapidly changing field of AI and NLP.

We will explore how it's changing everything from healthcare to education, business to creative arts, and beyond. We'll examine the future of job productivity and how we can prepare ourselves for the AI-augmented workforce.

So, buckle up for a thrilling ride into the future, and be prepared to change the way you think about technology, work, and communication. Welcome to the era of Conversations Not Code. Let the journey begin!

The dawn of AI can be traced back to the mid-20th century, with the seminal work of computing pioneers such as Alan Turing and John von Neumann. They envisioned machines that could not only compute but also 'think'.

Early AI focused on solving specific problems or executing certain tasks. These so-called expert systems were adept at their assigned tasks, but they lacked the flexibility and adaptability to handle unfamiliar situations.

Past: From Rules to Learning

AI experienced its first major shift with the advent of machine learning in the late 20th century. Instead of pre-programmed rules, machines began to 'learn' from data. This enabled them to handle a much wider range of tasks and adapt to new situations. Machine learning paved the way for significant advancements, including image recognition, speech recognition, and even autonomous vehicles.

Simultaneously, researchers began to explore how machines could understand and generate human language - a field known as Natural Language Processing (NLP). The first wave of NLP was dominated by rule-based systems, which, while effective at parsing rigidly structured language, struggled with the subtleties, ambiguities, and fluidity of natural human language.

Present: The Conversational Era

The present era of AI has been defined by a shift towards deep learning and neural networks, inspired by the architecture of the human brain. These models, combined with vast datasets and increasing computational power, have revolutionized NLP. Modern NLP systems, like OpenAI's GPT series, can generate incredibly human-like text, grasp context, and engage in meaningful dialogue.

The focus has shifted from the binary and rigid language of code to the more intuitive and accessible Conversations Not Code. Today, anyone can interact with AI using everyday language.

You can ask your virtual assistant to play a song, a business executive can request an AI to analyze a dataset, or a doctor can seek help from an AI to diagnose a medical image.

Future: The AI-Augmented World

Looking ahead, the potential of Conversations Not Code is truly staggering. The next generation of AI will become even more integrated into our daily lives and workflows. We will converse with our devices, applications, and data as we do with a colleague or assistant.

Advancements in AI will enable even more nuanced understanding and generation of human language, bridging the gap between humans and machines. With the democratization of AI, it will become a ubiquitous tool, augmenting human capabilities across all disciplines and industries.

We're entering an era where AI will be our companion and collaborator, understanding us and helping us accomplish tasks with unprecedented efficiency.

This future of AI is not simply about machines becoming more human-like, but rather about humans and machines working together symbiotically, leveraging their respective strengths to achieve goals that were previously unimaginable.

This is the future that Conversations Not Code promises: an AI-augmented world, where technology amplifies our capabilities and liberates us from mundane tasks, allowing us to focus on what truly matters—creativity, problem-solving, and the uniquely human ability to dream and imagine.

It's a future that we are not merely passive observers of, but active creators and shapers. Let's embark on this journey together.

AI has transitioned from the realm of science fiction to an indispensable tool in our everyday lives. It is all around us, often working behind the scenes, invisible yet impactful. From our smartphones to our cars, from the internet to our appliances,

AI has quietly woven itself into the fabric of our daily existence. Let's take a tour of the transformative power of AI in our everyday life.

Personal Assistants

Perhaps the most visible and familiar example of AI is the digital personal assistant. Devices like Siri, Alexa, Google Assistant, and Cortana use advanced NLP algorithms to understand and respond to our verbal commands.

They set reminders, answer questions, play music, control smart home devices, and even tell jokes. They're an early but powerful illustration of the Conversations Not Code paradigm.

Navigation and Transportation

AI has revolutionized how we navigate our world. Services like Google Maps use AI to predict traffic and suggest the fastest routes. Rideshare apps like Uber and Lyft use AI to match drivers with riders, optimize routes, and set prices.

Autonomous vehicles, though still in their early days, promise to fundamentally reshape transportation, driven by advancements in AI.

Online Shopping and Entertainment

AI systems power recommendation engines on platforms like Amazon, Netflix, and Spotify, curating personalized lists of products, movies, or songs based on our preferences and past behavior. These platforms use machine learning to analyze vast amounts of data and predict what we might like, enhancing our shopping and entertainment experiences.

Health and Fitness

AI has made inroads into our personal health and fitness routines as well. Fitness trackers and smartwatches use AI to monitor our activity, sleep, and other health indicators, providing personalized insights and recommendations. AI-powered apps can guide our workouts, help us meditate, and even monitor our mental health.

Communication and Work

AI helps us communicate more effectively, with email filters sorting our messages, spam detectors protecting us from unwanted emails, and predictive text speeding up our typing. In our professional lives, AI tools help us schedule meetings, automate repetitive tasks, analyze data, and much more.

The Future Everyday Life with AI

Looking forward, AI promises to become an even more integral part of our daily lives. We will converse with our devices and applications more naturally and intuitively, using our own language rather than coded commands. Our homes, cars, workplaces, and cities will become smarter and more responsive, understanding and anticipating our needs.

Through Conversations Not Code, AI will become more accessible and widespread, creating a future where everyone, regardless of their technical skills, can harness the power of AI. In this future, AI is not a distant, impersonal machine, but a helpful, responsive companion that enhances our capabilities and enriches our everyday lives.

We are standing at the threshold of a profound transformation in our relationship with technology. This change is being fueled by the confluence of advancements in artificial intelligence (AI), particularly in the field of Natural Language Processing (NLP).

We are transitioning from an era where interaction with digital systems required specialized knowledge and skills, to one where we can communicate with technology using the same language we use to talk to each other. Welcome to the era of Conversations Not Code.

Bridging the Gap

The foundational shift in Conversations Not Code is about democratization. For decades, the power of computing was locked behind the barrier of coding knowledge. If you didn't speak the language of machines, your ability to leverage their power was limited. Conversations Not Code aims to bridge this gap, making interaction with technology as simple and intuitive as having a conversation.

Ubiquity of Natural Language

One of the key reasons for the shift towards Conversations Not Code is the ubiquity of natural language. Regardless of our profession, education, or cultural background, we all know how to hold a conversation. By using natural language as the interface, AI can become a tool for everyone, not just those with specialized skills or training.

Enhanced User Experience

AI models trained on large datasets can understand and respond to a wide range of inputs, making the interaction with digital systems more flexible and natural. Conversations Not Code offers a more engaging, intuitive, and user-friendly experience, whether you're asking a virtual assistant to play your favorite song, or you're a doctor seeking an AI's assistance in diagnosing a complex case.

Conversations that Learn

Beyond their ability to understand and respond, advanced AI systems can also learn from conversations. Every interaction is an opportunity to refine and personalize the system's responses.

This ability for continuous learning and adaptation makes Conversations Not Code a powerful tool for personalization and enhancement of user experiences across platforms.

Future Prospects

The future prospects of Conversations Not Code are endless. As AI becomes more sophisticated, so will its understanding and generation of natural language. We're heading towards a future where we'll have detailed discussions with AI about complex subjects, where AI will help us solve intricate problems, generate creative ideas, and even offer emotional support.

This is the new era we are stepping into - an era where anyone can leverage the power of AI in their everyday lives, using nothing but their own language. It's a future that is more inclusive, more democratic, and more exciting. Welcome to the era of Conversations Not Code.

UNDERSTANDING A.I. & NATURAL LANGUAGE PROCESSING

In order to fully appreciate the impact of Conversations Not Code, it's essential to understand the foundational concepts of Artificial Intelligence (AI) and Natural Language Processing (NLP).

Artificial Intelligence (AI) is a broad branch of computer science that focuses on creating machines or software capable of performing tasks that typically require human intelligence.

These tasks include learning from experience, understanding complex concepts, recognizing patterns, interpreting and responding to language, and making decisions.

AI can be categorized into two types: Narrow AI and General AI. Narrow AI is designed to perform specific tasks, such as recommending a song on Spotify or identifying spam in your email inbox. It operates under a limited set of constraints and is very good at the tasks it's designed for.

On the other hand, General AI refers to systems or devices that can handle any intellectual task that a human being can. As of my knowledge cutoff in 2021, General AI remains largely theoretical.

Machine Learning (ML), a subset of AI, involves the creation of algorithms that allow computers to learn from and make decisions or predictions based on data.

Deep Learning, a further subset of ML, takes inspiration from the human brain in processing data, using layers of artificial neural networks to extract higher-level features from raw input.

Natural Language Processing (NLP) is a subset of AI that focuses on the interaction between computers and humans through language. It allows machines to understand, interpret, generate, and respond to human language in a valuable way.

NLP is at the heart of services like Google Translate, voice-operated assistants, and chatbots.

NLP can be divided into two main components: Natural Language Understanding (NLU) and Natural Language Generation (NLG). NLU involves the comprehension of language, including tasks like sentiment analysis, named entity recognition, and semantic parsing. NLG, on the other hand, is about generating coherent and contextually relevant sentences.

Conversational AI, the technology behind virtual assistants and chatbots, is a product of advancements in NLP. It allows users to interact with machines using natural language, whether spoken or written. Conversational AI has been integral in fostering the Conversations Not Code paradigm.

The combination of AI and NLP has the potential to revolutionize human-computer interaction. With Conversations Not Code, we're moving away from explicit, rigid commands towards an interface that understands and responds to our natural language. This synergy of AI and NLP promises to make technology more accessible, intuitive, and personal, empowering users and transforming industries across the board.

Basics of Artificial Intelligence

Artificial Intelligence (AI) is an exciting and transformative field that's reshaping everything from our daily routines to the global economy. However, understanding its principles is fundamental to fully grasping the impact of this technology. Here, we delve into the basics of AI, from its origins and types to the critical concepts of machine learning and deep learning.

What is Artificial Intelligence?

At its core, Artificial Intelligence is a branch of computer science that aims to create machines or software capable of exhibiting intelligence. This involves replicating or simulating human intelligence in machines, creating systems capable of learning from experience, understanding complex concepts, recognizing patterns, interpreting language, and making decisions.

Types of AI: Narrow AI vs. General AI

AI can broadly be classified into two categories:

Narrow AI

Also known as Weak AI, these are systems designed to perform a narrow task, and they operate under a limited set of constraints. Examples of Narrow AI include recommendation systems (like Netflix or YouTube), spam filters in email systems, voice assistants like Alexa or Siri, and customer service chatbots. These AI systems are exceptionally proficient at the specific tasks they're designed for.

General AI

Also known as Strong AI, these are systems or devices that possess the ability to perform any intellectual task that a human being can. They can understand, learn, adapt, and implement knowledge from one domain into another. As of my knowledge cutoff in 2021, General AI remains largely theoretical and is the subject of ongoing research.

Machine Learning: Teaching Computers to Learn

Machine Learning (ML) is a critical subset of AI that focuses on developing algorithms that allow computers to learn from and make decisions or predictions based on data. The key here is that the systems learn from data, identify patterns, and make decisions with minimal human intervention. ML is widely used in various applications including web search results, real-time ads, credit scoring, fraud detection, and recommendation systems.

Deep Learning: Mimicking the Human Brain

Deep Learning, a further subset of machine learning, utilizes artificial neural networks with several layers - 'deep' networks. It's inspired by the structure and function of the human brain, specifically the interconnections between neurons. These networks are excellent at recognizing patterns and are used in applications such as image and speech recognition.

In the era of Conversations Not Code, AI, particularly machine learning and deep learning, are critical as they drive the ability for computer systems to understand, generate, and respond to human language. Understanding the basics of AI helps us appreciate the sophistication, potential, and ethical considerations involved in this transformative technology. The next chapters will delve further into how this AI technology interfaces with natural language, forming the core of our conversation-based future.

Natural Language Processing Explained

As we progress further into the era of Conversations Not Code, the importance of understanding Natural Language Processing (NLP) becomes increasingly apparent. This chapter sheds light on NLP's significance, its key components, and how it brings us closer to seamless interaction with artificial intelligence.

What is Natural Language Processing?

Natural Language Processing (NLP) is a fascinating subfield of artificial intelligence that focuses on the interaction between computers and humans using natural language. The ultimate goal of NLP is to enable machines to understand, interpret, generate, and respond to human language in a way that is both meaningful and useful.

Components of NLP: Understanding and Generation

NLP is composed of two key components: Natural Language Understanding (NLU) and Natural Language Generation (NLG).

Natural Language Understanding (NLU): This is the process by which machines are able to comprehend and interpret human language. NLU involves complex tasks such as sentiment analysis (identifying if the text's sentiment is positive, negative, or neutral), named entity recognition (identifying persons, organizations, locations in the text), and semantic parsing (extracting structured meaning from sentences).

Natural Language Generation (NLG): This is the process through which computers generate human language, taking structured data and converting it into text. This can range from simple tasks such as generating a weather report from meteorological data to more complex ones such as drafting articles or producing summaries.

NLP in the Era of Conversational AI

The developments in NLP have been instrumental in paving the way for Conversational AI – the technology that powers the voice assistants, chatbots, and messaging apps we increasingly interact with today. These systems can understand human language inputs (thanks to NLU), generate human-like responses (thanks to NLG), and maintain a contextual conversation with the user.

The Power of NLP

When AI and NLP combine, they unlock the potential for machines to understand the nuances of human language, including slang, idioms, cultural nuances, and even errors in language use. This capability is transformative; it allows us to interface with technology using our natural language, paving the way for Conversations Not Code.

From simple tasks like asking a digital assistant about the weather to complex interactions like instructing a software to analyze a dataset and generate insights, NLP makes these interactions possible in a simple, conversational manner. As we continue to improve and refine our NLP technologies, we're making strides toward a future where the barrier between humans and machines becomes increasingly blurred.

The Power of AI-NLP Synergy

One of the most potent combinations in the world of technology today is that of Artificial Intelligence (AI) and Natural Language Processing (NLP). Together, they form the bedrock of our transition into the era of Conversations Not Code. This chapter will highlight the transformative power of this synergy and its potential impact on our interaction with technology.

Breakdown of Barriers

Traditionally, human-computer interaction has been constrained by the need for humans to understand the 'language' of machines—code. With the advent of Conversations Not Code, this is no longer necessary. Thanks to the synergy of AI and NLP, we're now able to interact with technology using our most natural form of communication: human language.

Democratization of Technology

This combination of AI and NLP is democratizing access to technology. In the past, using advanced software or applications required specific technical skills or understanding. Today, anyone who can speak or write can harness the power of AI through natural language interfaces. This broadens the user base of AI technologies and encourages their application in diverse fields.

Personalized Experiences

AI-NLP synergy doesn't just make technology more accessible; it also enhances the user experience. AI models, trained on vast amounts of data, can generate responses that are not only contextually accurate but also tailored to individual users. This level of personalization elevates the quality of interaction, making it more engaging and effective.

Seamless Integration

The fusion of AI and NLP allows for the seamless integration of technology into our daily lives. Whether it's a virtual assistant managing our schedules, a chatbot providing customer support, or an AI tutor aiding in learning, these technologies blend naturally into our routines, improving efficiency and productivity.

Accelerated Innovation

Lastly, the AI-NLP synergy accelerates innovation across industries. From healthcare and education to finance and entertainment, Conversations Not Code enables the development of new tools, services, and solutions that can address complex challenges and open up novel opportunities.

The synergy between AI and NLP is driving a seismic shift in the way we interact with technology. As we continue to advance in this field, we move closer to a future where technology understands us as we do each other, where we converse instead of code, and where the benefits of AI are not locked behind a barrier of technical expertise but are accessible to all through the power of language.

NLP PROMPT ENGINEERING: THE ART AND SCIENCE

One of the most exciting developments in the world of AI and NLP is Prompt Engineering. As we move forward into the Conversations Not Code era, understanding and leveraging prompt engineering becomes crucial for utilizing AI to its full potential.

In this chapter, we delve into the art and science behind it, illuminating the vast opportunities it presents.

Prompt Engineering refers to the art of crafting effective prompts or queries that are used to instruct AI models.

A well-designed prompt can effectively guide the AI's response, enabling it to generate more accurate, informative, and creative outputs. It's akin to asking the right questions to get the right answers.

Prompt Engineering is grounded in understanding how AI models process and respond to input. By gaining insights into the model's training, capabilities, and limitations, we can devise prompts that are well-aligned with its inherent processing mechanism, leading to better results.

On the other hand, the art of prompt engineering lies in designing queries that effectively communicate the desired task to the AI.

This requires a careful consideration of the task's context, the needed information, and the preferred format of the output.

The craft of prompt engineering lies in encapsulating all these factors into a succinct, clear, and effective prompt. The opportunities in prompt engineering are manifold. Here are just a few:

Improving AI Interactions: A well-crafted prompt can significantly improve the quality of interaction with AI, making it more engaging, productive, and user-friendly.

Enhancing AI Applications: By creating effective prompts, we can enhance the performance of AI applications in fields like customer support, content creation, data analysis, tutoring, and more.

Developing New Tools and Services: Prompt engineering opens up new possibilities for developing tools and services that harness the power of AI. From conversation design tools to personalized AI tutors, the possibilities are vast.

Empowering Non-Technical Users: With prompt engineering, non-technical users can effectively leverage advanced AI models for their needs. By learning to ask the right questions, they can unlock the power of AI without needing to understand the underlying code.

As AI models continue to evolve, so will the field of prompt engineering. In the future, we can look forward to more sophisticated prompts that can instruct AI to carry out complex tasks, multi-step processes, and even tasks that require a deep understanding of context or abstract concepts.

NLP Prompt Engineering is a pivotal skill in the Conversations Not Code era, acting as a bridge between human needs and AI capabilities.

By mastering this art and science, from online schools like the renown NLP Engineering Academy, we can unlock the full potential of AI, opening up a world of possibilities for innovation, efficiency, and growth.

Evolution of NLP Prompt Engineering

To fully appreciate the advent of Conversations Not Code, it's important to understand the evolution of programming languages, from the rudimentary machine languages to today's internet languages.

This journey serves as the backdrop for the rise of Natural Language Processing (NLP) and the subsequent emergence of Prompt Engineering. Here we embark on this historical journey and explore the evolution that led us to this transformative era.

Machine Language and Assembly Language: The Beginnings

The genesis of programming languages lies in Machine Language, the most fundamental form of programming. These languages used binary codes to instruct computers, making them difficult for humans to read and write.

To simplify this process, Assembly Language was created. These languages replaced binary codes with more human-readable mnemonics. However, programming in assembly was still a tedious task, requiring detailed knowledge of the computer's architecture.

Scripting Languages: A Leap Forward

Scripting languages, or high-level languages, represented a significant leap forward.

They used syntax and commands closer to human language, greatly simplifying the programming process. Languages such as Python, JavaScript, and Ruby fall into this category. They abstract away many low-level details, enabling programmers to write more complex programs efficiently.

Internet Languages:
Paving the Way for Interconnectivity

As the internet evolved, so did the need for languages that could handle the web's complexities. HTML, CSS, and JavaScript became the cornerstone for web development, allowing for the creation of dynamic and interactive web pages. On the server-side, languages like PHP, Python, and Java were used to handle data processing, database management, and server-client communication.

The Rise of
Natural Language Processing

While all these languages have eased human-computer interaction, they still required users to learn and understand their syntax and semantics. This is where Natural Language Processing (NLP) comes into the picture. NLP, a subfield of AI, focuses on the interaction between humans and computers using natural, human language. This eliminated the need for understanding programming languages and opened up the possibility of instructing computers using everyday language.

Evolution of NLP Prompt Engineering

Prompt Engineering represents the next step in the evolution of human-computer interaction. In this model, instead of using formal programming languages, users 'prompt' the AI model to perform tasks using natural language. For instance, instead of writing a complex script to analyze data, one might simply ask the AI, "What are the key trends in this data?"

This evolution of NLP Prompt Engineering marks a paradigm shift in our interaction with technology. It removes barriers to technology use, democratizes access, and makes human-computer interaction more natural and intuitive. As we continue to refine this process, the promise of Conversations Not Code brings us closer to a future where the power of AI is unlocked not by coding, but by conversation.

Techniques and Best Practices

As we move deeper into the era of Conversations Not Code, it's crucial to arm ourselves with techniques and best practices that can help us effectively interact with AI models using NLP.

This highlights some of these key strategies, offering insights into how we can harness the power of AI in our everyday tasks, across various fields, with more ease and efficiency.

Understanding the AI's Capabilities

AI models, though impressive, are not omnipotent. Understanding what the AI is trained on, what it can do, and what its limitations are, is essential. This awareness will help you formulate prompts that are in line with the model's capabilities, ensuring effective outcomes.

Precision in Communication

While AI models are capable of understanding natural language, clarity and precision in your prompts can significantly enhance the results. Be specific about what you want the AI to do and provide as much relevant information as possible.

Utilizing Templates

For regular tasks, creating and utilizing prompt templates can be beneficial. These are standard prompt structures that can be used consistently for similar tasks, requiring only minor modifications depending on the specific requirements.

Incremental Interaction

Engage with the AI incrementally, especially for complex tasks. Instead of trying to accomplish everything in one go, break down the task into smaller, manageable parts. This iterative approach can improve the AI's accuracy and make the task more manageable for you.

Continuous Learning and Adaptation

AI models learn from their interactions and improve over time. Likewise, we should also be open to learning and adapting. This includes understanding better how to communicate with the AI, identifying its strengths and weaknesses, and continuously refining our prompts.

Privacy and Ethics Consideration

While interacting with AI, it's important to remember the ethical and privacy implications. Ensure that sensitive information is not shared inappropriately and respect guidelines set for ethical usage of AI.

The era of Conversations Not Code calls for new skills and approaches. The ability to effectively prompt an AI model can significantly enhance our productivity and efficiency.

By understanding these techniques and best practices, we can navigate this exciting era with greater confidence and competence, unlocking the full potential of AI in our lives.

The Role of Prompt Engineering in A.I. Development

As AI continues to revolutionize various sectors and industries, the art of prompt engineering has become an integral part of AI development. It plays a key role in shaping how AI models interact with users, influencing their effectiveness and usability. In this chapter, we explore the role of prompt engineering in AI development, illuminating its transformative impact.

Prompt engineering is crucial in shaping the interaction between users and AI. A well-crafted prompt can guide the AI to generate more accurate, contextually relevant, and useful outputs. This results in more effective and engaging interactions, enhancing the overall user experience.

Prompts are not just about eliciting the right response; they also play a role in guiding the learning of AI models. They provide a form of supervision, helping models learn to focus on relevant information and understand the structure and context of human language better.

Through prompt engineering, we can democratize access to AI technologies. By enabling interaction through natural language, we open up AI technologies to a broader audience. This is especially relevant in the era of Conversations Not Code, where one doesn't need technical expertise to harness the power of AI.

Prompt engineering also plays a vital role in enhancing AI applications. Whether it's customer service chatbots, virtual assistants, AI tutors, or data analysis tools, effective prompts ensure these applications perform their tasks accurately and efficiently.

Lastly, prompt engineering shapes the development of AI models themselves.

The feedback and insights gained from the interaction between users and AI via prompts inform further improvements in AI models, making them more responsive and effective.

Prompt engineering is integral to the development and deployment of AI. As we continue to innovate and evolve in this space, the role of prompt engineering will become even more significant, guiding us towards a future where AI is more accessible, effective, and integrated into our daily lives.

A.I.
IN DIFFERENT FIELDS

Artificial Intelligence is not a technology of the future; it's here now, and it's revolutionizing a multitude of fields. From healthcare to education, entertainment to finance, the implications are profound and far-reaching.

In this chapter, we explore the impact of AI across different fields, specifically in the context of Conversations Not Code.

In healthcare, AI is aiding in everything from disease diagnosis to personalized treatment plans. Through Conversations Not Code, doctors can get real-time insights from vast medical databases, patients can receive tailored health advice, and public health organizations can monitor and respond to disease outbreaks more effectively.

AI is transforming education by offering personalized learning experiences and making education more accessible. Teachers can use AI to understand individual learning patterns and tailor their teaching methods. Students can interact with AI tutors through natural language, getting help on a range of subjects anytime, anywhere.

AI is revolutionizing the finance industry by automating complex processes, detecting fraud, managing risk, and providing personalized financial advice.

With Conversations Not Code, financial professionals can extract insights from vast datasets, customers can interact with AI assistants to manage their finances, and businesses can make more informed decisions.

In the entertainment industry, AI is being used for content recommendation, game development, virtual reality, and more.

Through Conversations Not Code, creators can collaborate with AI to generate content, users can interact with AI characters in games, and audiences can have more personalized entertainment experiences.

In retail, AI is enhancing the shopping experience, managing inventory, predicting trends, and improving customer service. With Conversations Not Code, customers can have conversational interactions with AI shopping assistants, and retailers can gain insights from their data to optimize their operations and strategy.

AI is making a significant impact across various fields. By marrying AI with NLP in the form of Conversations Not Code, we are democratizing access to these powerful technologies and opening up new possibilities for innovation, efficiency, and growth. As we look to the future, we can expect this influence to deepen and expand, reshaping our world in profound ways.

Healthcare

Artificial Intelligence is set to transform healthcare in unprecedented ways. As we navigate through the era of Conversations Not Code, we can expect this transformation to be even more profound, making healthcare more personalized, efficient, and accessible.

Personalized Medicine

AI will drive the shift from a one-size-fits-all model of healthcare to personalized medicine. Using vast amounts of data from various sources like genomic sequencing and health records, AI can help identify individual health risks and customize treatment plans. With Conversations Not Code, this can be done in real-time, providing instant insights to healthcare providers.

Intelligent Diagnosis

AI will play a pivotal role in disease diagnosis. It can analyze images, lab reports, and patient history to detect signs of disease. With advancements in NLP, these AI models can be prompted by doctors to focus on specific symptoms or patient data, leading to faster and more accurate diagnoses.

Virtual Health Assistants

AI-powered virtual health assistants will become common, offering health advice, monitoring patient's conditions, and even providing emotional support. With the power of Conversations Not Code, these interactions will be more natural and intuitive, allowing users to ask health-related questions or express their concerns in everyday language.

Drug Discovery and Development

AI will expedite the drug discovery and development process. It can analyze vast datasets to identify potential drug candidates and predict their effects.

Using natural language prompts, scientists can guide these AI models to focus on specific diseases, targets, or drug properties, leading to more targeted and efficient drug development.

Preventative Healthcare

AI will enable a more preventative approach to healthcare. By analyzing data on lifestyle, genetics, and environmental factors, AI can predict health risks and suggest preventive measures.

Through Conversations Not Code, individuals can easily interact with these AI models, gaining insights into their health risks and receiving personalized advice.

The future of AI in healthcare promises exciting advancements that can revolutionize the way we approach health and wellness.

As Conversations Not Code becomes the norm, we can expect these advancements to be more accessible, leading to a healthcare system that is more in tune with individual needs, proactive in its approach, and effective in its outcomes.

The future of healthcare is not just about more advanced technology, but about technology that is more human-centric, empathetic, and in sync with our needs.

Education

As we progress into the future, AI's role in education is set to be transformative. The integration of Conversations Not Code into the educational landscape will facilitate personalized learning experiences, foster inclusivity, and create more efficient teaching methodologies. In this chapter, we explore the exciting possibilities that lie ahead in AI-enhanced education.

Personalized Learning

In the future, AI will fully personalize the learning experience, tailoring it to each student's unique needs and learning style. Conversations Not Code will play a central role here.

AI will adapt to the student's pace, provide customized resources, and offer real-time feedback, all through a natural language interface that makes learning more interactive and engaging.

AI Tutors

AI-powered tutors will become more prevalent, accessible, and advanced. These virtual tutors can offer 24/7 assistance, providing immediate help on a wide range of subjects.

With the power of natural language processing, these interactions will feel more conversational and less robotic, enhancing the learning experience.

Inclusive Education

AI holds the promise of a more inclusive educational landscape. By removing barriers related to language, disability, and geographical location, AI can make quality education accessible to all. Conversations Not Code will play a pivotal role here, enabling more intuitive, accommodating, and adaptive learning environments.

Data-Driven Insights

AI will help educators gain data-driven insights into student performance, learning patterns, and curriculum effectiveness. This can guide teachers in adapting their teaching methods, identifying students who may need extra help, and refining curriculum design. With Conversations Not Code, these insights can be obtained easily and intuitively, right at the moment of need.

Lifelong Learning

AI will also facilitate lifelong learning, enabling individuals to learn new skills or subjects at any stage of life.

AI platforms will offer personalized learning pathways, career advice, and support through Conversations Not Code, making learning a continuous, accessible, and enjoyable journey.

The future of AI in education is bright, promising a revolution in how we teach and learn.

As we move further into the era of Conversations Not Code, these advancements will become more accessible and intuitive, paving the way for a more personalized, inclusive, and effective educational landscape.

With AI, we have the opportunity to reshape education for the better, creating a system that caters to every learner and fosters a lifelong love for learning.

Business & Finance

The intersection of AI and business is already changing the landscape of finance and commerce, driving innovation, efficiency, and growth.

As we step into the future, the incorporation of Conversations Not Code will augment these changes even further. This chapter explores how AI will shape the future of business and finance.

AI will play a pivotal role in improving business decision making. By analyzing vast amounts of data, AI can provide insights into market trends, consumer behavior, and operational efficiencies. With Conversations Not Code, these insights can be accessed easily, making data-driven decision making more accessible and intuitive.

From fraud detection to risk assessment to portfolio management, AI will automate a range of financial processes. Conversations Not Code will enable financial professionals to interact with these AI systems seamlessly, allowing them to focus on strategic tasks while AI handles the repetitive tasks.

AI will enable businesses to offer personalized experiences to their customers. This could be through AI-powered recommendations, tailored marketing messages, or personalized customer support. Conversations Not Code will play a crucial role here, allowing businesses to interact with their customers in a more human-like, personalized manner.

AI will drive operational efficiency by automating repetitive tasks, optimizing supply chains, and improving resource allocation. Through Conversations Not Code, businesses can easily interact with these AI systems, enabling them to optimize their operations in real-time.

AI will drive innovation and enable new business models. Whether it's AI-powered products and services or AI-driven business processes, the possibilities are endless. Conversations Not Code will make it easier for businesses to adopt and integrate these AI technologies, opening up new avenues for growth and innovation.

The future of AI in business and finance is exciting and transformative. As we embrace the era of Conversations

Not Code, these changes will become more accessible and intuitive. Businesses that harness the power of AI will not only become more efficient and competitive but also foster innovation, deliver superior customer experiences, and drive growth.

The future of business is not just about adopting advanced technology, but about leveraging it in a way that aligns with human needs and aspirations.

Creative Arts

Artificial intelligence is increasingly becoming a tool for creativity, expanding the horizons of art, music, literature, and more. As we continue our journey into the era of Conversations Not Code, this influence will only grow stronger. In this chapter, we explore the future impact of AI on the creative arts.

Art and Design

AI algorithms will continue to push the boundaries of art and design. From generating unique artwork to aiding in complex design processes, AI can unlock new avenues for creativity.

With Conversations Not Code, artists and designers can guide AI's creative process using natural language, making the interaction more intuitive and the output more in line with their vision.

Music and Sound

AI will play a transformative role in music creation and sound design. AI can compose music, create new sounds, and even learn and mimic specific music styles.

Through Conversations Not Code, musicians and sound designers can instruct and interact with these AI systems, fostering a new kind of creative collaboration.

Literature and Writing

AI will have a significant impact on literature and writing. AI can generate stories, poems, and even scripts, offering a new tool for writers.

With Conversations Not Code, writers can direct the AI in a conversational manner, making the process of co-creation more seamless and engaging.

Film and Animation

AI will revolutionize film and animation. From generating realistic CGI to automating the animation process to predicting viewer preferences, AI can enhance various aspects of film production. Conversations Not Code will enable filmmakers to interact with AI tools more naturally, shaping their creative output more effectively.

Performance Arts

AI will also find its place in performance arts. It can choreograph dances, direct theater performances, or even participate as an AI performer.

The adoption of Conversations Not Code will facilitate a more dynamic interaction between human performers and AI, leading to innovative performances that push the boundaries of traditional art.

The future of AI in the creative arts is exhilarating. As we advance into the era of Conversations Not Code, we will see a fusion of human creativity and AI capabilities, leading to a whole new realm of artistic expression.

AI will not replace human creativity, but rather augment it, pushing the boundaries of what's possible in the creative arts. The future holds an exciting convergence of art and technology, where AI becomes a canvas for our creative spirit.

Research & Development

Artificial Intelligence is set to become a driving force in Research & Development (R&D) across various fields.

As we move deeper into the era of Conversations Not Code, this influence will be significantly magnified, leading to accelerated innovation and discovery. This chapter explores the potential future impact of AI on R&D.

AI will play a crucial role in accelerating scientific discovery. It can analyze vast amounts of data, make connections, and generate hypotheses, speeding up the process of scientific research.

With Conversations Not Code, researchers can interact with AI in a more intuitive way, directing its focus and extracting insights.

As we've seen in healthcare, AI will be instrumental in drug discovery and development. By analyzing biological data and existing scientific literature, AI can identify potential drug candidates and predict their effectiveness.

Conversations Not Code will enable scientists to guide this process more effectively, significantly accelerating drug development.

In material science, AI can predict the properties of new materials, simulate experiments, and guide the development of advanced materials.

Through Conversations Not Code, material scientists can instruct and interact with AI in a more intuitive manner, leading to more efficient and innovative material design.

AI will also play a significant role in climate and environmental research. It can analyze complex climate models, predict environmental trends, and help design sustainable solutions. Conversations Not Code will facilitate a more dynamic interaction with AI, allowing researchers to ask complex questions and receive actionable insights.

In fields like physics, mathematics, and philosophy, AI can aid in advancing theoretical research. It can process complex equations, generate new hypotheses, and even contribute to debates in philosophy. With Conversations Not Code, theoreticians can collaborate with AI more effectively, pushing the boundaries of human knowledge.

The future of AI in Research & Development holds the promise of accelerated discovery, deeper understanding, and more sustainable solutions.

As we embrace Conversations Not Code, these advancements will become more accessible, democratizing the process of innovation and discovery. In the fusion of human intelligence and AI, we find the potential to transcend our limitations and expand the horizons of our collective knowledge.

Law And
The Legal Profession

In the legal profession, AI is set to make a profound impact. It will significantly streamline legal processes, improve access to legal services, and even alter how legal decisions are made.

As we enter deeper into the era of Conversations Not Code, these changes are set to become even more transformative. This chapter will explore the future impact of AI on the field of law.

AI will revolutionize legal research. Through analyzing vast amounts of legal documents, case laws, and legislation, AI can deliver comprehensive legal insights in mere moments.

With Conversations Not Code, legal professionals can interact with AI tools conversationally, asking complex questions and receiving detailed, relevant answers.

AI will streamline the contract review and analysis process. By scanning through contracts, AI can highlight potential issues, suggest edits, and even predict the outcome of contract negotiations.

The use of Conversations Not Code will make this process more intuitive, enabling legal professionals to guide AI with natural language prompts.

AI will improve access to legal advice and assistance. AI-powered legal chatbots can provide basic legal advice, guide users through legal processes, and even draft simple legal documents.

With Conversations Not Code, these interactions will be more natural and accessible, breaking down barriers to legal services.

AI will provide predictive analytics for legal decision making. It can analyze past case law and predict the likely outcome of legal cases. Through Conversations Not Code, legal professionals can easily interact with these AI models, allowing them to make more informed decisions and strategies.

As AI becomes more integral to the legal field, new ethical considerations will arise.

This section will discuss issues related to transparency, bias, accountability, and privacy in the use of AI in law. As we navigate through the era of Conversations Not Code, these ethical discussions will become increasingly important in shaping a just legal landscape.

The future of AI in law is transformative. It will streamline legal processes, democratize access to legal services, and revolutionize legal decision making.

As we embrace the era of Conversations Not Code, these changes will be more intuitive and accessible, reshaping the legal landscape to be more efficient, inclusive, and just. The potential of AI in law is not just about augmenting legal processes, but about reimagining a legal system that is in sync with our evolving societal needs.

CONVERSATIONS NOT CODE
ACROSS PLATFORMS

In the age of digital ubiquity, platforms and technologies are diverse and abundant. As AI evolves, it's crucial to ensure that its power is harnessed across these various platforms in a manner that is user-friendly and accessible. This is where Conversations Not Code comes in, offering a universal way to interact with AI irrespective of the platform being used

Universal Accessibility

With Conversations Not Code, AI's capabilities become universally accessible. Regardless of the platform—be it a smartphone, a laptop, a smart home device, or an industry-specific software—users can interact with AI in the same intuitive, conversational manner. This opens up AI's benefits to a wider audience, breaking down barriers related to technical proficiency or familiarity with a specific platform.

Seamless User Experience

As users move between platforms—both digital and physical—they expect a consistent, seamless experience. Conversations Not Code enables this continuity, allowing users to interact with AI consistently across platforms. This ensures a smooth user experience and fosters user trust and engagement.

Platform-Specific Customizations

While Conversations Not Code provides a universal way to interact with AI, it doesn't preclude platform-specific customizations. By understanding the user's context, AI can tailor its responses to suit the specific platform and the user's unique needs on that platform. This allows for a user experience that is both consistent and customized.

Future-Proofing AI Interaction

As technology evolves, new platforms and interfaces will emerge. Conversations Not Code provides a future-proof way to interact with AI, as it's based on the most natural form of human communication: conversation.

This ensures that as platforms evolve, AI's benefits remain accessible and its interaction remains user-friendly.

Building a Conversational AI Ecosystem

With Conversations Not Code, we're not just building individual AI applications; we're building a conversational AI ecosystem.

An ecosystem where AI applications across platforms can interact with each other and with users in a seamless, intuitive manner, driving efficiency, innovation, and user satisfaction.

Conversations Not Code is crucial for harnessing AI's potential across platforms. It ensures universal accessibility, seamless user experience, platform-specific customizations, future-proof interaction, and a conversational AI ecosystem.

As we move further into the era of Conversations Not Code, these benefits will become increasingly apparent, making AI an integral, accessible, and user-friendly part of our daily lives across all platforms.

The future of AI is not just about advanced algorithms, but about making these algorithms accessible and beneficial to all, regardless of the platform they use.

From Programming to Conversing:
A Paradigm Shift

The advancement of AI and Natural Language Processing (NLP) has brought us to the brink of a major shift in how we interact with technology.

The traditional model of programming, defined by complex codes and syntax, is evolving into a more intuitive model based on conversations. In this chapter, we explore the significance of this paradigm shift from programming to conversing, and what it means for the future of AI.

Conversations Not Code democratizes technology by making AI accessible to everyone, irrespective of their programming skills. By interacting with AI in natural language, anyone can leverage its capabilities, breaking down barriers and fostering inclusivity.

Conversations Not Code enhances user experience by making interactions with AI more natural, intuitive, and engaging.

This not only reduces the learning curve but also strengthens the relationship between users and AI, paving the way for more efficient and personalized experiences.

Conversations Not Code allows users to communicate with AI in a more direct and efficient manner. By expressing commands, queries, or instructions in conversational language, users can get more done, faster. This results in increased productivity across various tasks and industries.

By shifting the focus from understanding complex code to conversing with AI, individuals can dedicate more time and mental resources towards creative thinking and problem-solving. This fosters innovation and drives advancements in various fields.

Conversations Not Code brings us a step closer to humanizing AI. By using our natural language, AI can understand not just the literal meaning of our words, but also the context and nuances, resulting in a more human-like interaction.

The shift from programming to conversing represents a significant evolution in our relationship with technology. Conversations Not Code ensures that the power of AI is within the reach of everyone, enhancing user experiences, increasing efficiency, fostering creativity, and making interactions with AI more human-like.

As we stand on the threshold of this exciting new era, the potential of what we can achieve with Conversations Not Code is boundless. The future of AI interaction isn't about typing code; it's about having a conversation.

NLP in Major Tech Platforms

As the Conversations Not Code paradigm takes root, major technology platforms are integrating NLP to enhance user experience and improve productivity.

This chapter offers an in-depth analysis of how these platforms are utilizing NLP, and how it's transforming the way users interact with their services.

Google's search engine, Google Assistant, and many of its other services leverage NLP to understand and process natural language queries. By making search more conversational, Google aims to make information retrieval more intuitive and personalized.

Amazon's Alexa, an AI-powered virtual assistant, uses NLP to comprehend and respond to voice commands. This has revolutionized the smart home industry, enabling users to control their devices using just their voice.

Apple's Siri leverages NLP to facilitate hands-free, conversational interaction with Apple devices. Siri's capabilities extend beyond simple command processing to providing personalized suggestions based on user interactions.

Microsoft's Cortana, as well as several features in Microsoft Office, utilize NLP. This enhances productivity by enabling natural language queries, automated content creation, and smart suggestions based on user behavior.

Facebook uses NLP for content moderation, sentiment analysis, and chatbot interactions. NLP helps Facebook understand user-generated content, enhancing user experience, and maintaining a safe, positive community environment.

OpenAI's GPT (Generative Pretrained Transformer) models, like GPT-3 and beyond, are designed to understand and generate human-like text.

These models pave the way for more advanced Conversations Not Code applications across various domains.

NLP is becoming an integral part of major tech platforms, improving user experience, accessibility, and productivity.

As we advance further into the era of Conversations Not Code, we can expect this trend to continue, with more sophisticated NLP applications enhancing our interaction with technology.

The future of tech platforms lies in making the interaction as natural and intuitive as a conversation, and NLP is the key to achieving this.

Adapting the New Interface: Best Practices

As we transition into the era of Conversations Not Code, it's important to adapt to this new interface effectively. This chapter outlines some best practices to facilitate this transition and leverage the power of conversational AI to its fullest.

When interacting with AI through natural language, prioritize clarity. Be specific about your needs or questions to help the AI provide accurate and relevant responses. While NLP is getting better at understanding nuances, clarity always helps.

As with any new interface, there's a learning curve to Conversations Not Code. Don't be afraid to experiment, ask different types of questions, and see how the AI responds. This will help you understand its capabilities and limitations better.

Unlike traditional code, natural language is heavily dependent on context. Keep this in mind when conversing with AI, providing sufficient context where necessary, and understanding how the AI uses context to interpret your prompts.

AI and NLP technologies are continuously learning and improving. If the AI doesn't understand your query or provides an incorrect response, be patient.

Providing feedback, where possible, can also help improve the system over time.

While Conversations Not Code can make many tasks easier, it's not always the right tool for every job.

Understand when it's more efficient to use traditional coding methods or other tools, and when to leverage the power of conversational AI.

Adapting to the new interface of Conversations Not Code involves a shift in how we approach interaction with technology.

By following these best practices, we can navigate this transition smoothly and leverage the benefits of conversational AI to enhance our productivity, creativity, and overall experience.

As we continue to learn and adapt, we're not just embracing a new interface, but a new way of thinking and engaging with technology that brings us closer to our AI counterparts.

The future is conversational, and adapting to this reality is the first step towards harnessing the full potential of AI.

A.I. AND
JOB PRODUCTIVITY

A.I.'s integration into the workplace marks a significant evolution in how we carry out tasks and responsibilities. This "great merger" of A.I. and job productivity is fundamentally reshaping various industries, with Conversations Not Code playing a critical role. In this chapter, we delve into the impact of this merger and its implications for the future of work.

A.I., particularly when coupled with Conversations Not Code, excels at automating routine tasks.

Whether it's scheduling meetings, sorting emails, or generating reports, A.I. can handle these tasks quickly and accurately, freeing up valuable time for employees to focus on more complex responsibilities.

A.I. systems can process vast amounts of data and provide insights in real-time. With the ease of Conversations Not Code, these insights become readily accessible, enhancing decision-making across various job roles, from managers and executives to frontline workers.

A.I. can provide personalized learning experiences, adjusting content based on individual performance and learning styles. Through Conversations Not Code, employees can interact with these learning systems in a more engaging, natural manner, enhancing their professional growth.

Conversational A.I. can streamline communication within organizations, from summarizing meeting minutes to providing real-time translations. This fosters collaboration, reduces misunderstandings, and makes workplace communication more efficient.

As we move forward, the synergy of humans and A.I. will define the future of jobs. Rather than replacing humans, A.I., through the interface of Conversations Not Code, will augment human capabilities, enhancing productivity, creativity, and decision-making.

The great merger of A.I. and job productivity is a game-changer for the world of work. Conversations Not Code plays a pivotal role in this merger, making A.I. more accessible and integrated in the workplace.

As we embrace this new paradigm, we stand at the cusp of a productivity revolution, where A.I. not only transforms how we work but also redefines what we can achieve.

Current Impact on Job Efficiency

The advent of Conversations Not Code is already making waves in the job market, enhancing efficiency and transforming the way we work. Its current impact is evident across numerous sectors and roles, reshaping the productivity landscape.

At its core, Conversations Not Code excels in automation. It relieves professionals from the burden of routine and monotonous tasks, such as scheduling meetings, managing inbox clutter, or handling customer inquiries.

By automating these tasks, employees can focus their efforts on tasks that require creativity, strategic thinking, and human judgement.

In addition to task automation, A.I., via Conversations Not Code, provides powerful tools for data analysis and decision-making. Executives can ask A.I. for business insights or forecasts, analysts can delve into complex data sets with simple queries, and even sales representatives can leverage A.I. to understand customer sentiments and preferences better.

This has led to more informed decision-making, helping businesses improve their performance and adapt quickly to market changes.

Conversational A.I. is also transforming the learning and development landscape. Employees can learn new skills or knowledge in a more personalized and interactive manner.

Whether it's an A.I. tutor helping an employee understand a new software tool, or an A.I. coach providing personalized feedback, Conversations Not Code is making learning more accessible and efficient.

Another area where Conversations Not Code is making a significant impact is communication. From summarizing meeting minutes to providing real-time translations, A.I. is streamlining communication and collaboration in the workplace.

This has led to more productive meetings, reduced misunderstandings, and fostered a more inclusive work environment.

Conversations Not Code is already enhancing job efficiency in multiple ways. By automating routine tasks, aiding decision-making, personalizing learning, and streamlining communication, it's not just changing how we work, but also boosting our productivity and job satisfaction.

As we continue to harness the power of Conversational A.I., we can look forward to a future where technology and humans work in synergy, driving unprecedented levels of efficiency and innovation.

Predicted Transformations

As the era of Conversations Not Code matures, we stand on the precipice of a future full of exciting transformations. A.I. is poised to influence job productivity in ways that are likely to surpass even our most audacious predictions today.

One significant transformation we foresee is the ubiquitous presence of A.I.-powered personal assistants.

These intelligent helpers, capable of understanding and responding to natural language, will offload many of our routine tasks, manage our schedules, and even assist in complex problem-solving, making our work lives more organized and efficient.

Real-time insights will become an integral part of decision-making processes across sectors. Whether you're a CEO needing a quick business forecast, a scientist needing real-time data analysis, or a teacher looking for personalized educational content, A.I., through Conversations Not Code, will provide the answers swiftly and accurately.

Data-driven decisions will no longer require complex programming or data science skills, as A.I. breaks down these barriers.

Continuous learning and upskilling will become easier and more personalized. A.I. will transform learning and development from a static, one-size-fits-all approach to an adaptive, individual-centric experience.

Whether it's learning a new language or mastering a new tool, A.I. will guide us, adjust to our pace, and answer our queries in real-time.

A.I. will not only be a tool but will become a collaborative partner. It will work alongside us, augmenting our abilities, and helping us solve complex problems.

The synergy of human creativity and A.I.'s computational power will unlock new possibilities and solutions.

Finally, as A.I. takes over routine tasks, new jobs and roles will emerge. These roles will not only require human skills like creativity, empathy, and leadership, but also an understanding of how to interact with A.I., and how to harness its potential to enhance our capabilities.

In essence, the future of A.I. and job productivity is bound to bring transformative changes, making work more efficient, engaging, and dynamic.

As we master the language of Conversations Not Code, we're paving the way for a future where A.I. is not a threat but a powerful ally, enhancing our productivity and creativity in ways we're just beginning to imagine.

Preparing for the
A.I.-Augmented Workforce

In the evolving landscape of the A.I.-augmented workforce, the role of prompt engineering, a key facet of Conversations Not Code, has become increasingly vital.

As we transition into an era where human capabilities are enhanced by A.I., effective communication with A.I. systems becomes as critical as the A.I. capabilities themselves. This is where prompt engineering plays a crucial role.

Prompt engineering enables us to translate human language into instructions that A.I. can understand and act upon. It's the bridge that connects human intuition and A.I. efficiency. With well-crafted prompts, we can instruct A.I. to perform complex tasks, analyze vast amounts of data, generate insights, and even engage in creative endeavors.

Moreover, prompt engineering encourages a two-way communication with A.I., turning A.I. systems from mere tools into collaborative partners.

As we master prompt engineering, we can ask A.I. systems for explanations, challenge their decisions, and learn from their insights. This interactivity makes A.I. systems more than just passive tools—it turns them into active participants that can contribute to problem-solving and decision-making.

As part of preparing for an A.I.-augmented workforce, we need to focus on improving our skills in prompt engineering.

This doesn't mean that everyone needs to become an expert, but a basic understanding of how to interact with A.I. effectively can significantly boost productivity and efficiency.

As A.I. systems become more advanced, the ability to create effective prompts will allow us to leverage A.I. capabilities to their fullest.

Additionally, learning prompt engineering can facilitate a smoother transition into the A.I.-augmented workforce. As A.I. takes over routine tasks, the ability to instruct A.I. effectively becomes an essential skill.

Those who can leverage prompt engineering will be better equipped to adapt to the new work environment, where A.I. and humans work together.

As we prepare for the A.I.-augmented workforce, the importance of prompt engineering cannot be overstated. By mastering this art, with schools like the NLP Engineering Academy, we can communicate effectively with A.I., leverage its capabilities, and navigate the new era of work with confidence and proficiency.

As Conversations Not Code becomes the new norm, prompt engineering stands at the heart of this transformation, shaping our interactions with A.I. and determining how we harness its potential.

VII. PREPARING
FOR THE A.I. FUTURE

The future is one where AI intertwines seamlessly with our daily lives. In this future, Conversations Not Code is the language that allows us to unlock the potential of AI, making it accessible, understandable, and manageable for all. Here's how we can prepare for this future.

The first step towards preparing for an AI future is understanding AI's capabilities and limitations. While AI can process vast amounts of data and provide insights faster than any human could, it lacks the emotional intelligence and creativity inherent in humans. Understanding this enables us to identify where AI can add value and where human judgement is irreplaceable.

Next, we need to develop fluency in Conversations Not Code. This means not only understanding how to interact with AI but also how to instruct it effectively.

Mastering the art of prompt engineering is key here, as it allows us to translate our needs and instructions into a language that AI can understand.

Beyond interacting with AI, we also need to learn how to interpret its outputs. As AI becomes more integrated into decision-making processes, the ability to evaluate AI's recommendations critically and combine them with human judgement becomes increasingly important.

We also need to prepare for a shift in job roles and responsibilities. As AI automates routine tasks, the value of human skills such as creativity, leadership, and emotional intelligence increases. Preparing for the AI future means honing these skills and learning to leverage AI to enhance them.

Lastly, we must address the ethical implications of AI. This includes ensuring that AI systems are transparent, fair, and accountable.

As part of Conversations Not Code, we need to be able to ask AI systems about their decision-making processes, challenge their decisions, and hold them accountable.

Preparing for the AI future with Conversations Not Code involves understanding AI's capabilities and limitations, mastering prompt engineering, learning to interpret AI's outputs, preparing for a shift in job roles, and addressing the ethical implications of AI.

As we navigate this journey, we'll not only be preparing for the AI future but shaping it to ensure it benefits us all.

The Skillset for an AI-Driven World

As AI becomes increasingly woven into the fabric of our lives and work, the importance of mastering a new skillset defined by Conversations Not Code becomes paramount. This skillset empowers individuals to communicate with AI, leverage its capabilities, and ultimately thrive in an AI-driven world.

The first skill in this set is understanding AI. A basic comprehension of AI capabilities, principles, and limitations is essential to use AI effectively. This does not necessitate a deep technical understanding, but rather a familiarity with what AI can and can't do, and how it can augment human capabilities.

The second skill is prompt engineering. Being able to effectively craft prompts that translate our needs into a form AI can understand is at the heart of Conversations Not Code. This requires an understanding of how AI interprets language, an ability to break down complex tasks into simple instructions, and creativity to ask questions that can generate insightful outputs.

Interpreting AI outputs is another critical skill. AI can provide valuable insights, but it is up to humans to interpret these outputs, understand their implications, and use them to inform decision-making. This involves a degree of critical thinking, problem-solving, and decision-making skills.

The ability to learn from AI and improve over time is another essential skill. Conversations Not Code fosters a two-way communication with AI, allowing us to learn from AI's insights and improve our prompts based on AI's responses.

This continuous learning and improvement mindset is crucial to fully leverage the potential of AI.

Ethical awareness is another key component of the Conversations Not Code skillset. As AI is increasingly used in decision-making, understanding the ethical implications, including biases in AI systems and privacy considerations, is essential. This requires a degree of empathy, fairness, and responsibility.

The Conversations Not Code skillset for an AI-driven world includes understanding AI, prompt engineering, interpreting AI outputs, continuous learning, and ethical awareness.

By mastering this skillset, individuals can fully leverage the capabilities of AI, navigate the challenges posed by AI, and contribute to a future where AI works for the benefit of all.

Organizations and AI Transformation

In the realm of organizational operations, the advent of AI brings about a significant transformation. Fueled by the concept of Conversations Not Code, AI's role in business has escalated from being a niche, specialist tool to an organization-wide resource that can empower every employee, regardless of their coding proficiency.

Organizations can harness AI's power to analyze vast datasets, identify patterns, generate insights, and make predictions, thus driving data-driven decisions at an unprecedented scale and speed. This translates into improved business intelligence, predictive analytics, and strategic decision-making.

With Conversations Not Code, employees can interact with AI platforms in a natural, intuitive way, leading to the democratization of AI capabilities across the organization.

Beyond data analysis, AI can automate routine, time-consuming tasks, enabling organizations to operate more efficiently and employees to focus on strategic, creative, and interpersonal aspects of their roles.

In areas such as customer service, human resources, and administration, the automation of repetitive tasks not only improves efficiency but also enhances accuracy and consistency.

AI-driven transformation also fosters innovation within organizations. It opens new possibilities for product development, service delivery, and problem-solving, encouraging a culture of innovation and continuous improvement.

By enabling broader engagement with AI, Conversations Not Code facilitates a more inclusive and diverse innovation process.

However, this transformation is not just about leveraging AI; it's also about preparing the workforce for an AI-augmented future.

As AI takes over routine tasks, the value of human skills such as creativity, critical thinking, and emotional intelligence increases. Organizations must invest in reskilling and upskilling their workforce to navigate this new landscape successfully.

Ethical considerations are another critical aspect of this transformation. Organizations must address issues related to privacy, fairness, transparency, and accountability as they integrate AI into their operations.

Conversations Not Code enables more transparent AI systems as it allows users to ask AI about its decision-making processes, challenge its decisions, and hold it accountable.

The AI transformation offers immense opportunities for organizations. It has the potential to improve efficiency, foster innovation, and transform the workforce. However, it also brings new responsibilities.

By embracing Conversations Not Code, organizations can ensure they leverage AI's benefits responsibly and equitably, driving their growth while also contributing to a more inclusive and ethical AI-driven world.

Conversation Not Code:
Educating the Next Generation

In the rapidly evolving world of technology, Conversations Not Code emerges as an essential element of AI literacy that needs to be incorporated into the education of the next generation.

This approach shifts the focus from traditional, code-intensive programming to a more accessible, conversational engagement with AI, thereby democratizing its use and benefits.

Education plays a crucial role in preparing students for a future increasingly shaped by AI. However, rather than focusing solely on traditional coding skills, the emphasis needs to shift to fostering an understanding of AI, its capabilities, and ethical implications, alongside mastering the art of interacting with AI through conversation.

Conversations Not Code empowers students to engage with AI in a more intuitive, human-like manner. It leverages the most natural form of human communication – conversation – to instruct and interact with AI systems. This approach makes AI more approachable, allowing students to harness its power without needing advanced coding skills.

In the classroom, this can take the form of students using AI as a tool to support their learning. For example, they might use an AI-powered system to find information, solve problems, or receive personalized learning support.

Through interacting with AI in this way, students can better understand AI's capabilities and limitations, develop critical thinking skills as they interpret AI's outputs, and learn to use AI as a tool to augment their learning.

Moreover, by learning to use AI through conversation, students develop valuable skills for the future workforce. They learn to break down complex problems into smaller, manageable tasks that AI can assist with, a skill that mirrors the problem-solving and project management skills required in many jobs. They also develop skills in critical thinking and decision-making as they learn to evaluate AI's suggestions and use them to inform their decisions.

However, Conversations Not Code is not just about using AI; it's also about understanding the ethical implications of AI. As part of their education, students need to understand the biases that can be inherent in AI systems, the importance of privacy, and the need for transparency and accountability in AI decision-making.

Integrating Conversations Not Code into curricula paves the way for an educational transformation. Traditional rote learning gives way to experiential learning scenarios where students get to witness the immediate impact of their interactions with AI, fostering curiosity and enhancing their understanding of the technology.

This could be facilitated through AI-powered educational games, simulations, and problem-solving activities that require students to provide input and instructions to AI in a conversational manner.

In addition to enhancing student engagement, the Conversations Not Code approach promotes inclusivity in AI education.

By removing the technical barriers associated with coding, more students, irrespective of their background or academic strengths, can participate in AI-enhanced learning experiences.

This could have a significant impact on reducing the digital divide and ensuring that the benefits of AI are accessible to all students.

Teachers play a vital role in this transformation. They would need to familiarize themselves with AI tools and the concept of Conversations Not Code.

Professional development programs can equip teachers with the skills and knowledge to integrate AI into their teaching and guide students in their interactions with AI.

The education system also has a responsibility to prepare students for a workforce that will be increasingly automated. Conversations Not Code promotes skills that will be invaluable in the future, such as creativity, empathy, critical thinking, and adaptability.

These skills, along with an understanding of AI and how to interact with it, will help future professionals excel in an AI-augmented workforce.

However, with the integration of AI into education, schools must also consider ethical and privacy concerns. It's important for schools to establish clear policies on data privacy and to educate students on responsible AI use.

Ultimately, the Conversations Not Code approach to AI education can help students not only to thrive in a future dominated by AI but also to shape this future.

The Conversations Not Code approach to AI education is about empowering the next generation to harness the potential of AI while also preparing them to navigate the ethical challenges it poses.

By incorporating this into education, we can prepare students for a future where AI is an integral part of work and life, ensuring they have the skills and knowledge to use it responsibly and effectively.

VIII.
CASE STUDIES

Case Study 1:
Streamlining Healthcare
Through Conversational A.I.

In a leading hospital, Conversations Not Code paved the way for a patient-centered, efficient healthcare system. They employed an A.I.-powered conversational interface to automate patient intake and follow-ups, freeing up staff to focus on providing care.

The system uses NLP to understand patients' descriptions of their symptoms, ask pertinent questions, and provide initial assessments. It also aids in maintaining medical records, scheduling appointments, and sending reminders, providing a seamless healthcare experience.

Case Study 2:
Enhancing Education
Through A.I. Tutoring

A high school in a suburban district transformed its learning approach using Conversations Not Code. They introduced an A.I.-powered tutoring system capable of answering students' queries, providing personalized learning resources, and identifying gaps in understanding.

By communicating with the A.I. through natural language, students were able to actively engage in their learning process, which resulted in improved academic performance and increased interest in the subject matter.

Case Study 3:
Boosting Efficiency
in the Retail Sector

A multinational retail corporation used Conversations Not Code to improve its inventory management. They employed a conversational A.I. system to handle inquiries about stock availability, ordering, and tracking, which previously required manual intervention. The A.I. system responded to employees' instructions and queries in natural language, reducing the time spent on inventory management and enabling employees to focus on customer service and sales.

Case Study 4:
Revolutionizing Market Research
Through Conversational A.I.

A global market research firm adopted Conversations Not Code to automate the analysis of consumer sentiment. Instead of manually sifting through customer reviews, their analysts used a conversational A.I. system to extract insights. By simply asking the A.I. system questions in natural language, analysts could gain insights into customer preferences, trends, and potential issues. This not only saved time but also provided deeper, more nuanced insights.

Case Study 5:
Empowering Public Service
Through Conversational A.I.

A city council employed Conversations Not Code to provide better services to its citizens. A conversational A.I. system was set up to answer queries about city services, process complaints, and provide information about city events. By interacting with this system in natural language, both city staff and citizens could access information quickly and efficiently, improving the overall effectiveness of city services.

Case Study 6:
Enhancing Agricultural Practices

A medium-sized farm incorporated Conversations Not Code into its farming practices. The farmers used an A.I. system capable of monitoring weather patterns, soil conditions, and crop health. By interacting with this A.I. in natural language, they could ask for real-time updates, forecasts, and advice on farming practices. This not only increased their crop yield but also led to more sustainable farming practices.

Case Study 7:
Transforming Non-Profit Operations

A non-profit organization serving underprivileged communities employed Conversations Not Code to streamline its operations. The organization used a conversational A.I. to manage donor databases, track donations, and coordinate volunteer efforts. The ease of interacting with the A.I. system in a conversational manner improved efficiency and enabled the organization to better serve its communities.

Case Study 8:
Optimizing Transportation and Logistics

A major transportation and logistics company integrated Conversations Not Code into its operations. The company used a conversational A.I. system to manage bookings, handle inquiries, and provide real-time updates on package delivery. The conversational interface enabled staff members to manage these tasks more efficiently, improving customer service and boosting overall productivity.

Case Study 9:
Improving Customer Service
in Banking

A multinational bank adopted Conversations Not Code to improve its customer service. The bank employed a conversational A.I. system capable of handling customer inquiries, assisting with transactions, and providing personalized financial advice.

By communicating with the A.I. through natural language, customers had access to round-the-clock service, improving customer satisfaction and retention.

Case Study 10:
Promoting Sustainability
in Urban Planning

A local government used Conversations Not Code in its urban planning initiatives. Using a conversational A.I. system, city planners could access data on traffic patterns, public transport usage, and environmental impact metrics. The ease of asking questions and receiving responses in natural language helped the planners make more informed, sustainable decisions.

These case studies underline the versatility and transformative potential of Conversations Not Code. Regardless of the sector or industry, a conversational interface with A.I. can unlock new efficiencies, enable smarter decision-making, and ultimately pave the way for innovation and growth.

These case studies demonstrate the transformative power of Conversations Not Code across different sectors. By making A.I. more accessible and intuitive, Conversations Not Code can optimize operations, enhance services, and empower both employees and customers.

Successful Implementations of A.I. NLP

In the world of customer service, Conversations Not Code has revolutionized the way companies interact with their customers. A.I.-powered chatbots, capable of understanding natural language, can now respond to queries, provide information, and solve problems in real-time. This has not only improved the customer experience but has also allowed businesses to offer 24/7 support.

In personal computing, virtual personal assistants like Siri, Alexa, and Google Assistant are standout examples of successful implementation.

Their ability to understand and respond to voice commands has made technology more accessible and user-friendly.

From setting alarms and playing music to controlling smart home devices, these intelligent assistants have brought Conversations Not Code into our homes.

Translation services have also benefitted from Conversations Not Code. Services like Google Translate use A.I. NLP to interpret and translate text in various languages, enabling communication and understanding across linguistic barriers.

Meanwhile, in the realm of market research and social media, Conversations Not Code has been used to develop A.I. models capable of sentiment analysis.

These systems can analyze vast amounts of data, such as customer feedback and social media posts, to identify trends and gain insights, guiding business strategies and product development.

The healthcare sector has seen successful implementations of Conversations Not Code in diagnostic tools. A.I. systems, like Babylon Health's A.I. doctor, can understand patients' descriptions of their symptoms, suggest possible diagnoses, and recommend next steps. This has opened the door to more accessible healthcare options.

Organizations across sectors are using Conversations Not Code to automate reporting. A.I. models can understand and interpret complex data, extracting key insights, and present them in a user-friendly, conversational manner. This has streamlined the often time-consuming process of data analysis.

In the manufacturing sector, Conversations Not Code has been employed in the form of conversational interfaces that help automate processes and manage machinery.

Operators can interact with the A.I. using natural language, issuing commands and receiving status updates, making it easier to control complex operations and improve productivity.

In the entertainment and e-commerce sectors, A.I. systems using NLP have been deployed to provide personalized recommendations. By understanding the preferences of users, these systems offer recommendations based on prior interactions.

Platforms like Netflix and Amazon are well-known examples of this implementation, with users getting customized content and product suggestions.

Mental health support has also seen the benefits of Conversations Not Code, with therapeutic chatbots like Woebot offering cognitive behavioral therapy through a conversational interface. These bots converse with users in a non-judgmental, supportive manner, helping to provide immediate mental health support at any time.

In human resources, A.I.-powered chatbots have been successfully deployed for recruitment and employee engagement. These bots can screen resumes, schedule interviews, answer FAQs, and even conduct initial interviews, reducing the workload on HR teams. In addition, they can also collect and analyze employee feedback in a conversational way, fostering better engagement.

Conversations Not Code is also transforming journalism with A.I. systems like Wordsmith that can automatically generate news stories from data.

By inputting data about a sports game or financial report, these systems can create a well-written article, freeing up journalists to focus on more complex, investigative work.

In disaster management and crisis response, Conversations Not Code has enabled the creation of A.I. systems that can provide critical information, assist in coordinating relief efforts, and offer support to those affected.

These A.I. interfaces can understand and respond to queries, providing real-time help during emergencies.

These diverse examples emphasize the transformative potential of Conversations Not Code. By enabling more natural interaction with technology, it allows A.I. and NLP to be applied in more contexts, making these advanced technologies more accessible and user-friendly.

Our everyday writing has been enhanced by Conversations Not Code with the development of predictive text and autocorrection features. These A.I. models understand the context of our text, predict our intended words, and correct our typos in real-time, making digital communication faster and more efficient.

In all these instances, the implementation of A.I. NLP with Conversations Not Code has made technology more accessible, efficient, and user-friendly, highlighting its transformative potential across various domains.

Lessons Learned from A.I. NLP Failures

Lesson 1:
The Limits of Rule-Based Systems

Early A.I. NLP systems often relied on rigid, rule-based systems which led to poor user experiences due to their inability to understand nuanced or context-dependent language.

These systems demonstrated that without the flexibility of Conversations Not Code, A.I. NLP applications can fail to understand and respond accurately to users' inputs.

Lesson 2:
The Challenge of Cultural and
Linguistic Diversity

Several A.I. NLP applications have faced criticism for their inability to cater to diverse cultural and linguistic contexts. This has highlighted the importance of adopting Conversations Not Code, which encourages building systems capable of understanding and interacting with a broad range of languages, dialects, and colloquial expressions.

Lesson 3:
Ignoring User Experience

A common pitfall for A.I. NLP applications has been overlooking the importance of user experience. Without the use of Conversations Not Code, A.I. systems can become a set of complex commands and operations that are hard to navigate for average users. This has reiterated the need for a conversational, user-friendly interface.

Lesson 4:
Overemphasis on Technology
Underemphasis on Utility

Some A.I. NLP failures resulted from an overemphasis on the technology's capabilities while neglecting its utility. Without a focus on Conversations Not Code, these applications often developed features that, while technologically impressive, did not enhance the system's usability or meet the users' needs.

Lesson 5:
Inability to Handle Ambiguity

Language is often ambiguous, with the same words or phrases meaning different things in different contexts. A.I. NLP applications that have not utilized Conversations Not Code have frequently struggled with this aspect of natural language, leading to misunderstandings and incorrect responses.

Lesson 6:
Neglecting the Importance
of Continuous Learning

A.I. systems, particularly those dealing with language, should be designed to learn and adapt over time. Failure to incorporate this element, and not utilizing Conversations Not Code, has led to systems becoming outdated or irrelevant. Systems must be designed to evolve with changing languages, slang, and cultural contexts to remain useful and relevant.

Lesson 7:
Lack of Empathy and Emotional Intelligence

Many A.I. NLP systems that haven't employed Conversations Not Code approach failed to exhibit empathy or understand emotional nuances in conversations.

This has made interactions with these systems feel impersonal and robotic, leading to a poor user experience.

Lesson 8:
Overlooking Privacy and Security Concerns

In several instances, NLP systems without Conversations Not Code have been associated with breaches of privacy, as they failed to adequately anonymize and secure user data.

This points to the importance of building conversational A.I. systems with robust security measures to protect sensitive user information.

Lesson 9:
The Challenge of Sarcasm and Humor

A.I. NLP systems not leveraging Conversations Not Code often struggle with interpreting sarcasm, humor, or idioms, leading to misunderstanding or miscommunication.

This reveals the importance of building systems capable of comprehending more than just the literal meaning of words.

Lesson 10:
Failing to Provide Context-Aware Responses

Many A.I. NLP applications failed to provide context-aware responses due to their inability to maintain a conversational context over a period of time.

This lack of contextual understanding often results in disjointed and irrelevant responses, thereby impairing the conversational experience.

By acknowledging these failures and the lessons they provide, we can better understand the importance of adopting the Conversations Not Code approach.

It is vital to ensure that A.I. NLP systems are designed to be adaptable, empathetic, secure, context-aware, and capable of understanding the complexities of human language. These lessons highlight the critical importance of Conversations Not Code in the development and application of A.I. NLP systems.

By focusing on a conversational, natural language-based Conversations Not Code approach, we can utilize A.I. applications that are more intuitive, accessible, and effective in a range of contexts.

The Future: Promising A.I. Projects in Development

As we look toward the horizon of artificial intelligence, the integration of Conversations Not Code into future projects paints a vivid picture of progress and potential.

Across industries and research domains, the future of A.I. is being shaped by innovative initiatives that use natural language interfaces to make technology more accessible, personalized, and intuitive.

In linguistics, for instance, we're seeing a surge of interest in creating multilingual A.I. models. The aim is to break down language barriers and bring A.I.'s transformative power to every corner of the globe, enabling people to communicate with A.I. models in their native tongue, be it a global language or a local dialect.

This democratization of language access could revolutionize everything from education and healthcare to business and governance.

Meanwhile, strides are being made to enhance A.I.'s ability to understand the context of conversations. Rather than simply processing one-off commands or queries, the next generation of A.I. models will be able to track the ebb and flow of an entire conversation, providing more relevant and insightful responses based on the evolving context.

In terms of emotional intelligence, researchers are developing A.I. models capable of perceiving and responding to the emotional undertones of human language.

This ability to exhibit empathy and emotional understanding will not only make interactions with A.I. more engaging and natural but could also unlock new applications in areas such as mental health support and customer service.

High-level abstract reasoning is another exciting frontier for A.I.. By equipping A.I. models with the ability to grasp complex concepts, draw inferences, and engage in intellectual debates, we could usher in an era of A.I.-powered research assistants, advisors, and even collaborators capable of contributing to scientific, philosophical, or strategic discussions.

Education is another sector ripe for transformation. A.I. models capable of adaptive learning, assessing a student's understanding and tailoring educational content to match their learning style and pace, promise to revolutionize how we teach and learn.

These models can provide personalized learning experiences that optimize each student's potential, all delivered through a friendly, conversational interface.

The future of A.I. also promises to respect our privacy. As the conversation around data privacy grows louder, developers are striving to create A.I. models that deliver personalized experiences without compromising personal data. Privacy-focused conversational A.I. is an emerging field that will shape how we interact with technology in a secure, privacy-respecting manner.

And finally, the creative industries are not immune to A.I.'s influence. The future may well see A.I. models that can understand, critique, and even generate art, music, and literature.

By leveraging Conversations Not Code, we could harness A.I.'s potential to not just consume but create original creative content, expanding the horizons of what's possible with machine intelligence.

This peek into the future, though far from exhaustive, illustrates the immense potential of Conversations Not Code approach in developing A.I. applications. The future of A.I. is a future of more natural, intuitive, and meaningful interactions - a future where conversations, not code, rule the day.

IX.
CONCLUSION

As we conclude this journey through the world of artificial intelligence, it becomes clear that we are at the threshold of a new era – the era of Conversations Not Code. Through the lens of A.I., we've seen how our relationship with technology has evolved and continues to evolve, shifting from complex coding and programming to a more natural, conversational interaction.

The impact of this shift is far-reaching, transforming every sector from healthcare and education to business, law, creative arts, and beyond. A.I. is not just an abstract concept or a tool for tech companies. It has become an integral part of our everyday lives, enhancing efficiency, driving productivity, and augmenting our capabilities.

Yet, at the heart of this transformative power is a simple yet profound shift: the move towards conversation. By adopting Conversations Not Code, we are humanizing A.I., making it more intuitive, accessible, and empathetic. We are enabling machines to understand us better, and in turn, empowering ourselves to harness the full potential of A.I..

However, the journey towards a future powered by Conversations Not Code is not without challenges. As we have learned from past failures, there is a need for continuous learning, better understanding of context and emotions, stronger privacy and security measures, and a constant focus on adaptability and inclusivity.

Preparation for this future is essential. This involves developing the right skillsets, adapting our educational systems, transforming our organizations, and most importantly, changing our mindset. We must move from viewing A.I. as an impersonal, complex technology to seeing it as an ally, a companion, a tool that we can converse with to solve problems and create value.

As we look ahead, we see a landscape filled with promising A.I. projects – multilingual models, emotionally intelligent A.I., context-aware systems, adaptive learning models, and creative A.I.. These developments offer a glimpse into a future where technology understands and interacts with us in the most natural way possible: through conversation.

In the end, the goal of Conversations Not Code is not just about improving our interaction with technology. It's about improving our lives. It's about making technology work for us, in the most human way possible. The future of A.I. is here, and it speaks our language.

With Conversations Not Code, we are creating a future where technology is no longer a complex, foreign entity, but a trusted companion, a facilitator of human potential, a part of our everyday conversations.

So, as we step into this future, let us remember: the future is Conversations Not Code.

The world stands at the cusp of an A.I. revolution, a shift in technology's role and capabilities that promises to reshape every aspect of human life. Yet, amidst the excitement and anticipation, there lies a fundamental challenge: How do we, as individuals and societies, effectively embrace this revolution? The answer lies in a profound yet intuitive paradigm shift - embracing Conversations Not Code.

For years, the primary method of interacting with digital technology was through interfaces that required us to adapt our behavior to the machine's needs. We had to learn specific commands, understand how software or algorithms work, or even learn to code. A.I., with its ability to learn, adapt, and mimic human behavior, represents a major shift in this relationship.

A.I. now presents the opportunity to converse with technology in the same way we do with fellow humans. The Conversations Not Code paradigm brings to life the promise of A.I.: technology that adapts to humans, not the other way around. It represents a shift from human-machine interaction to human-machine conversation.

Embracing the A.I. revolution with Conversations Not Code requires a three-fold approach:

1. Understanding the Language of A.I.: While Conversations Not Code reduces the need for technical expertise, a basic understanding of how A.I. works is still important. This understanding allows us to effectively communicate with A.I., utilize its capabilities, and also comprehend its limitations. It aids in building a beneficial and balanced relationship with A.I..

2. Adapting Our Mindsets: As A.I. becomes more integrated into our daily lives and workplaces, we need to shift our perspectives. We need to view A.I. not as a threat or a replacement but as a tool for augmentation. Embracing A.I. with Conversations Not Code is about leveraging A.I. to enhance our capabilities, improve our productivity, and create new opportunities.

3. Developing New Skills: The Conversations Not Code era requires new skills. These range from understanding and designing conversational interfaces to prompt engineering and empathetic design. As A.I. continues to advance, continual learning and skill adaptation become critical.

Embracing the A.I. revolution with Conversations Not Code is a transformative journey. It promises a future where technology is more human, where our interactions with machines are more natural and intuitive, and where the boundary between human intelligence and artificial intelligence blurs, opening up a realm of endless possibilities. It's about stepping into a future where we converse, collaborate, and create with A.I., making our lives, workplaces, and societies smarter, more efficient, and more connected.

In the era of Conversations Not Code, we're experiencing the initial stirrings of a profound transformation in our relationship with technology. The shift from traditional coding interfaces to conversational interactions with A.I. heralds a myriad of exciting opportunities that are expected to reshape our world.

1. Democratization of A.I. Technology: At the heart of the Conversations Not Code movement is the ambition to democratize access to A.I. technologies. As we evolve from complex coding systems to intuitive conversation-based interactions, A.I.'s capabilities become accessible to a wider audience. This expands the scope of who can use and create A.I., fostering a surge of innovation from diverse perspectives and backgrounds.

2. Enhanced Efficiency and Productivity: By fostering natural, human-like interaction, Conversations Not Code has the potential to drastically enhance efficiency and productivity across various industries. From healthcare to finance, education to law, the intuitive interface can help automate routine tasks, augment decision-making, and streamline complex workflows.

3. Personalized A.I. Experiences: Conversations Not Code paves the way for highly personalized A.I. experiences. With A.I.'s ability to understand and respond in human language, it can adapt to individual users' needs, preferences, and contexts, offering tailored services and solutions. This means more engaging, relevant, and efficient interactions across services, from digital assistants to customer support.

4. Empowered Creativity and Innovation: The conversational interface provides a natural platform for expressing ideas and exploring possibilities, fostering creativity and innovation.

Users from various fields can leverage A.I.'s analytical prowess to find patterns, generate insights, and drive creative problem solving.

5. Breakthroughs in Research and Discovery: Conversational A.I. has immense potential to accelerate research and discovery in various fields. By enabling researchers to interact with complex data sets through natural language, A.I. can support the discovery of new insights and understandings, paving the way for breakthroughs in science, medicine, and beyond.

6. Inclusive and Accessible Technology: Conversations Not Code offers the promise of a more inclusive and accessible technological landscape. By reducing reliance on complex codes and commands, conversational A.I. can make digital tools and services more accessible to people with disabilities, non-technical users, and people from different language backgrounds, promoting digital inclusivity.

7. Augmented Human Intelligence: Perhaps the most profound opportunity lies in A.I.'s potential to augment human intelligence. Conversations Not Code opens the door to a symbiotic relationship between humans and A.I., where A.I. serves as a cognitive collaborator, helping us make better decisions, spark new ideas, and unlock our full potential.

The era of Conversations Not Code promises a future where technology is more than just a tool—it's a collaborator, an assistant, a source of insight, and a facilitator of human potential. As we learn to converse with A.I., we pave the way for a future that is not just about making machines more intelligent but about amplifying human intelligence, creativity, and capacity to innovate.

The era of Conversations Not Code signals not just a technological shift but a societal one. It's about making the vast wealth of knowledge and the unprecedented computational capabilities of A.I. accessible to all, ushering in an era where every individual can stand on the shoulders of not just giants, but of all humanity.

The Conversations Not Code approach is democratizing A.I. in a manner that is truly transformative. No longer are the intricate, complex aspects of artificial intelligence the sole domain of a select few with years of technical training.

Now, anyone who can converse - can query, can ask, can express curiosity or problem-solving initiative - has the potential to tap into the collective knowledge and analytical prowess of artificial intelligence systems.

As we look to the future, we see an era where each conversation with A.I. brings us closer to the vast repository of human knowledge, experience, and wisdom. Your questions, be they about historical events, complex scientific concepts, philosophical dilemmas, or pragmatic problem-solving, can be met with comprehensive, informed responses distilled from a vast, global corpus of knowledge. Conversations Not Code is becoming the bridge between the individual and the collective wisdom of humanity, realized through the lens of A.I..

This does more than democratize access to knowledge. It democratizes problem-solving, innovation, and creativity. When every curious mind, regardless of background or resources, can tap into the wealth of human knowledge and computational capabilities of A.I., we expand the boundaries of what's possible.

We'll see innovations sparked from the most unexpected places, solutions to pressing problems emerging from minds that previously didn't have the tools to fully express their potential.

Moreover, Conversations Not Code brings us closer to a world where technology is inherently more inclusive. People from all walks of life, with varying degrees of technical expertise, different languages, and even those with physical disabilities, can tap into A.I.'s potential using the most natural tool at their disposal—their voice or their ability to converse.

The era of Conversations Not Code isn't merely an evolution in how we interact with technology—it's a revolution in accessibility, in democratizing knowledge, and in empowering humanity, with online schools like the renown NLP Engineering Academy, it heralds a future where every conversation holds the potential to unlock a world of knowledge and every individual is empowered to explore, innovate, and create.

X. APPENDIX – GLOSSARY

Adaptive Learning Systems: A.I. systems that can adapt and personalize the learning experience to cater to the individual needs, preferences, and progress of each learner.

A.I. Bias Mitigation: The process of identifying and addressing biases in A.I. systems to ensure fair and equitable outcomes, taking steps to reduce or eliminate biases that may be present in data, algorithms, or decision-making processes.

A.I. Integration: The process of incorporating A.I. technologies and systems into existing infrastructure, workflows, and applications, enabling organizations to leverage A.I. capabilities to enhance efficiency and productivity.

A.I. Model Deployment: The process of making trained A.I. models accessible and operational, enabling them to process user inputs and generate outputs or responses in real-time or near real-time scenarios.

A.I. Research Collaborations: Partnerships and collaborations between organizations, researchers, and institutions to advance the frontiers of A.I. technology through joint research, knowledge sharing, and resource pooling.

A.I. Trustworthiness: The measure of an A.I. system's reliability, transparency, and adherence to ethical principles, ensuring that users can have confidence in the system's behavior, decision-making, and data handling practices.

A.I.: Artificial Intelligence; the development of computer systems that can perform tasks requiring human intelligence, such as natural language processing and problem-solving.

A.I.-Assisted Decision-Making: The use of A.I. technologies to analyze large volumes of data, identify patterns, and provide insights that support human decision-making processes, leading to more informed and data-driven choices.

A.I.-Assisted Healthcare: The integration of A.I. technologies in healthcare settings to improve diagnostics, treatment planning, medical imaging analysis, patient monitoring, and drug discovery, enabling more accurate diagnoses, personalized care, and efficient healthcare delivery.

A.I.-Augmented Creativity: The use of A.I. technologies to enhance and augment human creativity in fields such as art, music, writing, and design, leveraging A.I.'s capabilities to generate novel ideas, assist in creative processes, and push the boundaries of artistic expression.

A.I.-Augmented Workforce: The concept of integrating A.I. technologies and capabilities into the workplace to enhance and augment human productivity and decision-making.

A.I.-Driven Decision Support: The use of A.I. technologies to assist humans in making informed decisions, providing insights, predictions, and recommendations based on data analysis and pattern recognition, ultimately improving decision-making processes across various domains.

A.I.-Driven Personalization: The use of A.I. technologies to tailor user experiences, content, and recommendations based on individual preferences, behaviors, and historical data, providing personalized and relevant interactions.

A.I.-Enabled Automation: The use of A.I. technologies to automate repetitive or time-consuming tasks, freeing up human resources for more complex and creative work, and increasing overall productivity.

A.I.-NLP Synergy: The synergistic relationship between Artificial Intelligence (A.I.) and Natural Language Processing (NLP), where A.I. systems leverage NLP techniques to understand, process, and generate human language.

A.I.-Powered Virtual Assistants: Digital assistants that utilize A.I. technologies to understand and respond to user queries and commands, providing personalized assistance and performing tasks on behalf of users.

Artificial Intelligence (A.I.): The development of computer systems that can perform tasks requiring human intelligence, such as natural language understanding, problem-solving, and learning.

Assembly Language: A low-level programming language that uses mnemonics to represent machine instructions and is specific to a particular computer architecture.

Bias: Systematic favoritism or prejudice in A.I. algorithms or datasets that can result in unfair or discriminatory outcomes, requiring careful mitigation to ensure fairness and equity.

Case Studies: Detailed examinations and analyses of specific instances or examples to understand and illustrate real-world applications and outcomes.

Contextual Understanding: The ability of A.I. systems to comprehend and interpret language within the context of a conversation or specific situation, taking into account previous interactions and information.

Conversational A.I. Platforms: Software frameworks or platforms that facilitate the development and deployment of conversational A.I. applications, providing tools and resources for building intelligent chatbots, virtual assistants, and voice-enabled interfaces.

Conversational UX Design: The practice of designing user experiences for conversational A.I. systems, focusing on creating intuitive, engaging, and seamless interactions that mimic human conversation and optimize user satisfaction.

Conversations Not Code Skillset: The collection of skills and competencies required to effectively utilize and interact with A.I. systems using Conversations Not Code principles.

Conversations Not Code: The paradigm shift in A.I. towards natural language interfaces, allowing users to interact with A.I. systems through conversation rather than traditional programming or coding.

Creative Arts: The field encompassing various forms of artistic expression, such as visual arts, music, literature, and performance, where A.I. is being increasingly explored as a tool for creation and inspiration.

Data Privacy: The protection and responsible handling of personal data collected by A.I. systems, ensuring compliance with privacy regulations and safeguarding individuals' privacy rights.

Emotionally Intelligent A.I.: A.I. systems that can recognize, interpret, and respond to human emotions, enabling more empathetic and personalized interactions.

Explainable A.I.: The capability of A.I. systems to provide clear and understandable explanations for their decisions, actions, or recommendations, enabling users to trust and comprehend the reasoning behind A.I.-generated outcomes.

Human-Centered A.I.: The approach to designing and developing A.I. systems that prioritize human needs, values, and well-being, aiming to create technology that enhances human experiences and respects human autonomy.

Human-Machine Collaboration: The concept of humans and A.I. systems working together in a cooperative and synergistic manner, leveraging the respective strengths and expertise of each to achieve optimal outcomes.

Internet Languages: Languages used in web development, such as HTML, CSS, and JavaScript, enabling the creation of interactive and dynamic web pages and applications.

Job Productivity: The level of efficiency, output, and effectiveness in performing tasks and responsibilities within a job role.

Knowledge Cutoff: The point in time until which the A.I. model has been trained and has knowledge. Information beyond this cutoff is not accessible to the A.I..

Law: The field of study and practice that deals with legal principles, regulations, and the application of rules in society, where A.I. is increasingly being utilized to support legal research, contract analysis, and other legal tasks.

Machine Language: Low-level programming languages directly understood by computers, consisting of binary instructions that control hardware operations.

Machine Learning: A subset of A.I. that involves training algorithms to learn patterns and make predictions or decisions based on data, without being explicitly programmed.

NLP (Natural Language Processing): The field of A.I. that focuses on enabling computers to understand, interpret, and generate human language, facilitating communication between humans and machines.

Privacy: The protection of personal information, ensuring that data collected by A.I. systems is handled securely, with respect for individual privacy rights and legal regulations.

Privacy-Focused Conversational A.I.: A.I. systems designed with a strong focus on protecting user privacy, ensuring that personal data is handled securely and used responsibly.

Prompt Engineering: The process of crafting specific instructions or queries to guide A.I. models in generating desired outputs or responses, ensuring the A.I. system understands user intent.

Prompt: A specific input or query provided to an A.I. model to generate desired outputs or responses.

Research and Development (R&D): The process of creating new knowledge, technology, or products through systematic investigation and experimentation.

Script Languages: High-level programming languages designed for specific applications or tasks, often utilizing prewritten scripts or code snippets for ease of use and rapid development.

Security: The measures taken to protect A.I. systems and data from unauthorized access, attacks, or breaches, ensuring the integrity, confidentiality, and availability of information.

Sentiment Analysis: The process of determining the emotional tone or sentiment expressed in text or speech, often used to understand public opinion, customer feedback, or social media sentiment.

Subchapters: Subsections within chapters that organize and provide structure to the content of a book.

Transparency: The principle of making A.I. systems understandable and explainable, ensuring that the decision-making processes and outcomes of A.I. algorithms are clear and can be audited or scrutinized.

User Experience (UX): The overall experience and satisfaction of users when interacting with A.I. systems, including factors such as ease of use, efficiency, and the quality of the interaction.

UX: User Experience; the overall experience and satisfaction of users when interacting with A.I. systems.